# ONCE UPON A WORLD

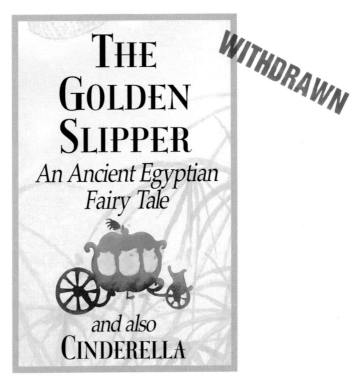

# THE GOLDEN SLIPPER

## An Ancient Egyptian Fairy Tale

*and also*
# CINDERELLA

## by SAVIOUR PIROTTA
## and ALAN MARKS

SEA-TO-SEA
*Mankato Collingwood London*

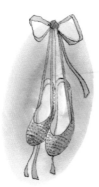

This edition first published in 2008 by
Sea-to-Sea Publications
1980 Lookout Drive
North Mankato
Minnesota 56003

Text copyright © Saviour Pirotta 2004, 2008
Illustrations copyright © Alan Marks 2004

Printed in China

Library of Congress Cataloging-in-Publication Data

Pirotta, Saviour.
  The golden slipper / by Saviour Pirotta and Alan Marks.
    p. cm. -- (Once upon a world)
  Summary: Presents two tales to compare and contrast, the first one from ancient Egypt
and the second one from France.
  ISBN 978-1-59771-077-0
  1. Fairy tales. [1. Fairy tales. 2. Folklore.] I. Marks, Alan, 1957- II. Title.

PZ8.P6672Go 2007
[398.2]--dc22

                                                2007060715


9 8 7 6 5 4 3 2

Published by arrangement with the Watts Publishing Group Ltd, London.

Editor: Rachel Cooke
Series design: Jonathan Hair

# Contents

# *Once upon a time*

*Cinderella* is undoubtedly one of the most popular fairytales in the world and comes in many different versions. The best-known one was written by the Frenchman Charles Perrault and you can read it at the end of this book. Variations exist in many countries and cultures, including North and South America, Eastern Europe, China, India, and the Middle East.

Every version has a magic helper who comes to the rescue of an ill-treated girl. Perrault's story features a fairy godmother. The brothers Grimm told a German variation where the helper is an enchanted tree. Other magic helpers include the Goddess of Mercy (Vietnam) and a talking bull (Norway). A black cow appears in a Himalayan version of the story, whose main character is a boy.

Not all the stories feature a slipper as a means of identification. In the Himalayan tale, the hero is recognized by a lock of golden hair. In a Russian story, the heroine is identified by a golden hairband, as well as a ring and a slipper, while her Indian counterpart gets to marry the king when he finds her nose ring.

However, *The Golden Slipper* does feature a slipper—and a magic helper in the form of a falcon. It was first told in ancient Egypt and written down by the Greek historian Strabo in the 1st century C.E. It is part fairytale, part legend because it features a king who really did exist. His name was Pharaoh Amasis II and he ruled Egypt in the 6th century B.C.E. He married a Greek slave called Rhodopis, who sounds very much like the girl in our story. So perhaps there really was a Cinderella, after all.

# The Golden Slipper

Once there was a Greek girl called Rhodopis.
Her mother had been a gifted dancer before
she died and Rhodopis was just like her. No
one in the village could dance with her grace
and elegance. She danced on the steps of the
temple to honor the goddess; she danced in
the market to earn some money; and she
danced around the olive groves to entertain
her friends during the harvest.

One day Rhodopis was dancing alone on
the beach. She was so busy with her feet,
she didn't notice two strange men pulling a
small boat up onto the sand behind her.

Suddenly, a rough hand was clasped over
her mouth and she was dragged, struggling
furiously, across the sand and into the boat.
Her captors pulled the boat back into the
water and, moments later, she was hauled
aboard a galley and thrown below deck. The
craft swiftly set sail. In the darkness of the
hold, Rhodopis realized what had happened:
she'd been taken by pirates!

The brigands did not let their captive out again until their galley had docked in a vast harbor filled with ships of every size and shape. As Rhodopis blinked in the sunlight, she saw more people than she'd ever seen in her life. They swarmed like ants along the quayside. "Where am I?" Rhodopis gasped.

"Egypt," came the short reply.

The pirates took her on shore to a slave market a little way from the harbor. There, after much haggling and shaking of fists, they sold Rhodopis to a wine merchant. Like her, he was Greek. His name was Charaxus.

Rhodopis's new master took her to his boat, which was piled high with amphorae of wine ready to sail up the Nile. A servant, half-blind and toothless, hoisted the sail and they traveled along the great river until they reached the bustling city of Naucratis.

Charaxus's home was a mansion, with
white walls and latticed windows looking
onto the river. Rhodopis was not surprised
to find other slaves there—three Egyptian
girls, with copper skin and eyes lined with
black kohl.

The slaves noticed immediately that the
newcomer had the same color skin and
eyes as Charaxus. She had the same hair, too,
although their master hid his under a wig.

"She must come from the same country as the master," whispered the eldest.

"She'll be his favorite then, even though she's the lowest in the household," moaned the second.

"We'll probably have to do all of her tasks," hissed the third.

And the three of them agreed, right there and then, to make Rhodopis's life a misery. That way she'd be sure to know her place.

"Milk the goats, you good-for-nothing," they commanded every morning.

"Clean out the hen run."

"Go and wash the laundry in the river."

If Charaxus had heard them ill-treating Rhodopis he would have stopped them. But he was hardly ever at home; his work took

him abroad for months on end.

Poor Rhodopis! How she wished she was back in her village, dancing on the steps of the temple or helping with the olive harvest. Now she had no home of her own, no belongings, and no friends to confide in. All she had left of her old life was her dancing.

She knew that the other slaves would take that away from her too, given half a chance. They would forbid her to dance. So she was careful to keep her talent a secret. She only danced when she was alone by the Nile, after she'd draped the laundry on the reeds to dry.

Now, one day, it so happened that
Charaxus was lying close to where
Rhodopis was hanging up the laundry.
He'd gone fishing and fallen asleep in
his boat. Rhodopis did not see him, for
his boat was masked by the reeds.
When she started dancing,
Charaxus woke up.
"What a graceful creature
Rhodopis is," he thought,
watching her leaping
and swaying.

The next time Charaxus was away, he remembered Rhodopis's dancing, and he bought her home a present: a pair of golden slippers made by a famous shoemaker in Athens. When the other slaves saw the golden slippers they were consumed with jealousy.

"The master has never bought us a present," complained the eldest.

"Not even a string of wooden beads," groaned the second.

"Or a hemp anklet," added the youngest.

And the three of them swore to treat Rhodopis even more harshly.

A few days later, they were standing
outside the hen run, making sure Rhodopis
cleaned every corner of it, when a messenger
arrived with important news. He was
dressed from head to toe in perfumed linen,
and his sandals were covered in jewels.

"His royal highness, the Pharaoh Amasis
the Second, ruler of Upper and Lower
Egypt, conqueror of all his enemies and

beloved of the gods, is holding open court at his palace in Memphis," he announced. "All the women in the land are invited, so that the king may choose a wife."

A wife! The pharaoh was looking for a wife! Charaxus's slaves, who thought themselves as beautiful as the morning sun, prepared to go to Memphis right away. One of them was sure to snare the pharaoh...

They made Rhodopis
bleach their linen robes;
they ordered new wigs
and cones of perfumed
wax to wear beneath them.
Charaxus was away in Samos.
He had taken the boat, so the slaves stole
money from his chest and hired a barge.

"Can I come too?" asked Rhodopis, as she helped them prepare. "I would like to see the pharaoh's court. Perhaps there will be dancers there, and musicians with harps."

"Of course!" replied the slave girls. "You must come." But they had no intention of taking Rhodopis with them. Imagine if the pharaoh preferred her to one of them!

So the wily
creatures sent
her to fetch
some food for the
journey. While she
was gone, they
hurried aboard the
barge.

"Make haste," they
commanded the
oarsmen. "It's a long
way to Memphis."

The vessel was already
in the middle of the river,
caught in the strong current,
when Rhodopis returned home
with the food.

"Don't forget to milk the goats,"
jeered one of the slaves across the water.

"And remember to feed the hens,"
sneered another.

"Or we'll be very angry with you," cackled the youngest. She was by far the most cruel of the three.

Rhodopis stood on the banks of the river, fighting back the tears. No, she would not give them the satisfaction of seeing her cry. She might never see the pharaoh's court but, with all three slaves away, she could dance all day now without fear
of punishment.

As the boat disappeared into the distance, Rhodopis put on the golden slippers. She'd been dancing for quite a while when she missed her footing and stumbled into the river. Mud oozed into one of the delicate slippers. 'Oh dear!' said Rhodopis. She took it off, washed it in clear water and set in on a rock.

While she was waiting for it to dry, she lay down on the sand to rest and fell asleep. Overhead, a falcon appeared, wings spread wide. It saw the slipper glinting in the sun and swooped down toward it. Rhodopis woke up to the flurry of wings. She leapt to her feet but it was too late. The falcon had already flown away, the slipper in its talons.

Later that evening, Pharaoh Amasis was
sitting in his lotus garden, flanked by courtiers
and scribes. The palace teemed with women
who had accepted his invitation. They had
come from all over Egypt, every one of them
trying to impress the pharaoh with her finery,
her talents, and her gracious manners.

"There are as many women in my
kingdom as there are stars in the heavens,"
thought the young Amasis, "but which one
would make the ideal queen of Egypt? And
me a happy husband? I like none I have
seen so far. If only the gods would help me
choose the right wife."

The pharaoh was about to rise, to go to the temple and consult with his priests, when something fell in his lap. A golden slipper!

Amasis looked up to see a falcon wheeling overhead. "It is a messenger from Horus," he thought to himself, "the falcon-headed god of protection."

An unearthly voice echoed in his head: "The woman whose foot fits into this golden slipper will be the one you can trust. She will be your queen."

The pharaoh stood up. The gods had answered his prayer. "My wife shall be the woman whose foot fits this slipper," he announced. And, just as Charaxus's slaves were being admitted into the palace, he dismissed the court.

News of the pharaoh's search spread through Egypt like the summer flood. All over the land, women dreamed of trying on the golden slipper, smiling in their sleep when it fitted them.

After a few weeks—it felt like an eternity to Charaxus's slaves—a royal barge reached Naucratis. The pharaoh was not on board but his vizier had brought the golden slipper. One by one, the women of the city tried it on, first the nobles, then the priestesses from the temple, and finally the commoners. It fitted no one.

At last the vizier approached Charaxus's house, where a large crowd had gathered. The merchant's Egyptian slaves were waiting by the door, itching to try on the slipper. Rhodopis was not with them, for they had locked her in the hen house.

The eldest tried the slipper on first.

"Alas," said the vizier, "your foot is too wide."

Then the second one tried it on. "What a pity," sighed the vizier, "your instep is rather too high."

Finally the youngest tried squeezing her foot into it. She was the most determined to make it fit, but to no avail.

"What a shame,' said the vizier, "your toes are too big."

He took the slipper back and addressed the crowd. "Is there anyone else who wants to try the golden slipper on?" he asked.

The slaves shook their heads. "No, no one," they chorused.

"Yes, there is," called out a voice behind
them. It was Charaxus, who had returned
home and freed Rhodopis from the hen
house. The vizier held out the golden slipper.

"Would you like to try it on?"

Rhodopis took the slipper and, of course,
her foot slipped into it right away.

"It fits," cheered the crowd. "It fits!"

Rhodopis produced the matching slipper
and put it on her other foot. The vizier
smiled, pleased that at long last his search
was over. "His royal majesty awaits you in
Memphis," he said. "Will you come?"

"I will," said Rhodopis.

"But your honor," shrieked the slaves, "Rhodopis is not even Egyptian. Take one of us. We're far more beautiful."

It was no use making a fuss. Rhodopis was already out of their reach, borne away by the royal barge. They wouldn't be able to torment her anymore…

Later in the year, after the floods had spread their fertile mud over the country, Rhodopis married Pharaoh Amasis the Second. She wore her golden slippers to the wedding, and she danced in them all night, to honor the goddess, to remember her dear mother, and to celebrate the beginning of her new life as the queen of Egypt.

# Cinderella

*When* Cinderella *was retold by Charles Perrault in 1697, he called it* The Little Glass Slipper, *although it is now better known by the name of its heroine. Perrault first heard the tale from local storytellers but he added many of the details that we love: the fairy godmother, the pumpkin carriage, and the glass slipper.*

Once there was a rich widower who married a cruel woman. No sooner was the wedding ceremony over than the new wife began to ill-treat his daughter. She forced her to do the meanest work in the house while her own two daughters did nothing all day but admire their reflections in the mirror.

The girl dared not tell her father about their cruelty, for she knew that he was blind to his new wife's faults. When she had done her work, she would sit

alone among the ashes and cinders in the chimney corner. Her stepsisters soon started to call her Cinderella.

It happened that the king's son was holding a ball—so grand that it was to last two nights. Cinderella's stepmother and sisters were invited, but they ensured Cinderella was not. On the happy day, they set off to the palace in their carriage, leaving Cinderella alone in the house.

Her godmother, who saw her crying bitterly, appeared and said, "My child, you wish that you could go to the ball; is it not so?"

"Yes," replied Cinderella.

"Then," said her godmother, who was a fairy, "run into the garden and bring me a pumpkin."

Cinderella went immediately to gather the finest pumpkin, and brought it to her godmother. The fairy struck it with her wand and it was instantly turned into a coach, gilded all over with gold.

The fairy then went to look in the mousetrap, where she found six mice. She gave each one a little tap with her wand, and each mouse was that moment turned into a fine horse. She found a rat in the rat trap too, and changed him into a jolly coachman with whiskers.

The fairy godmother then waved her wand at Cinderella and, in an instant, her clothes turned into a gown of gold and silver, all beset with jewels. This done, she gave Cinderella a pair of glass slippers. "Enjoy yourself my child," she said, "but do not stay at the ball past midnight or else the coach will be a pumpkin again, the horses mice, the coachman a rat, and your clothes mere rags once more."

Cinderella promised her godmother to be home by midnight and drove to the palace in her carriage. The king's son, who was told that a mysterious princess had arrived, ran out to meet her. He gave her his hand and led her into the hall.

All at once there was a hush in the room. Everyone stopped dancing and the violins ceased to play.

"How beautiful she is!" whispered the guests.

"Who is she?"

"Where does she live?"

The king's son asked Cinderella to dance with him. She moved so very gracefully that everyone admired her.

All too soon Cinderella heard the clock strike a quarter to twelve. She rushed out of the palace, flew into her carriage, and arrived home just before her sisters.

The next evening was the second night of the ball and, once again, Cinderella drove to

the palace. She enjoyed dancing with the king's son so much that she quite forgot the time and, before she knew it, the clock began to strike twelve.

Cinderella jumped up and fled, leaving on the steps of the palace one of her glass slippers, which the prince picked up most carefully. Cinderella reached home in her ragged old clothes, having nothing left of all her finery but the other glass slipper.

A few days later, the king's son proclaimed that he would marry the girl whose foot fitted into the glass slipper. His servants traveled around the country, trying it on first the princesses, then the duchesses, and finally on all the girls of humble birth.

At last the slipper was brought to Cinderella's two stepsisters, who did all they could to force their foot into it.

Cinderella was watching their struggles. "Let me see if it will fit my foot," she said.

Her sisters laughed but the gentleman who had brought the slipper said he had orders to allow everyone to try.

He asked Cinderella to sit down, and, putting the slipper to her foot, found that it went on very easily. Her two sisters were greatly astonished; they were more so when Cinderella pulled out of her pocket the other slipper, and put it on her other foot.

Then in came her godmother and touched her wand to Cinderella's clothes, making them richer and more magnificent even than the gown she had worn before.

And now her two sisters realized she was that beautiful lady who had danced with the prince. They threw themselves at Cinderella's feet to beg forgiveness for all the wrongs they had done her. Cinderella embraced them, saying that she forgave them with all her heart.

A few days later she married the prince. Her two sisters came to live with her in the palace and, that very same day, Cinderella matched them with two handsome lords of the court.

# Taking it further

Once you've read both stories in this book, there is lots more you can think and talk about. There's plenty to write about, too.

• To begin with, think about what is the same and what is different about the two stories. Talk about these with other people. Which story do you prefer and why?

• Make up your own story about a magic helper. Perhaps this could be a tree outside your school or house. It might be your favorite bird or animal. What magic powers would your helper possess?

• Retell *Cinderella* as a modern-day story set in your neighborhood. Where would Cinderella live? Would she go to school or to work? What kind of music would be played at the ball? Who would the guests be?

• Using the Internet, your library, and newspapers can you find any "real life" stories similar to *Cinderella*. How do these stories end? Talk about how real life differs from the world of fairytales.